Native American Library

INUIT
History and Culture

Helen Dwyer and Michael Burgan

Consultant Robert J. Conley
Sequoyah Distinguished Professor at Western Carolina University

Gareth Stevens
Publishing

Please visit our website, www.garethstevens.com. For a free color catalog of all our high-quality books, call toll free 1-800-542-2595 or fax 1-877-542-2596.

Library of Congress Cataloging-in-Publication Data

Burgan, Michael.
Inuit history and culture / Michael Burgan.
    p. cm. — (Native American library)
Includes bibliographical references and index.
ISBN 978-1-4339-5972-1 (pbk.)
ISBN 978-1-4339-5973-8 (6-pack)
ISBN 978-1-4339-5970-7 (library binding)
1. Inuit—History—Juvenile literature. 2. Inuit—Social life and customs—Juvenile literature. I. Burgan, Michael. Inuit. II. Title.
E99.E7B8895 2011
971.9004'9712—dc22

2010052209

New edition published in 2012 by
Gareth Stevens Publishing
111 East 14th Street, Suite 349
New York, NY 10003

First edition published 2005 by Gareth Stevens Publishing

Produced by Discovery Books
Project editor: Helen Dwyer
Designer and page production: Sabine Beaupré
Photo researchers: Tom Humphrey and Helen Dwyer
Maps: Stefan Chabluk

Photo credits: Cover Marilyn Angel Wynn/Nativestock.com/Getty Images; Ansgar Walk: p. 6; Corbis: pp. 10, 16, 17, 19 (top), 17 (both), 23, 26 (bottom), 28, 29, 30, 32, 36; Dmitrijsh: p. 5; Floyd Davidson: p. 39; Getty Images: pp. 31 (Kuba Morc/isifa), 33 (Richard Oisenius/National Geographic), 37 (Tom Hanson/AFP), 38 (Carlo Allegri/AFP); Native Stock: pp. 8, 14 (bottom), 20, 22, 26 (top), 27; Peter Newark's American Pictures: pp. 11, 13, 14 (top), 15, 19 (bottom); Shutterstock: pp. 24 (Achim Baque), 25 (AleksandrN), 34 (Jan Martin Will); The SilentPhotographer at en.wikipedia: p. 35.

Printed in the United States of America

CPSIA compliance information: Batch #CS11GS: For further information contact Gareth Stevens, New York, New York at 1-800-542-2595.

CONTENTS

Words that appear in the glossary are printed in **boldface** type the first time they appear in the text.

INTRODUCTION

THE INUITS IN NATIVE AMERICAN HISTORY

The Inuit are a people who inhabit the **Arctic** and **subarctic** regions of Siberia, Alaska, Canada, and Greenland. They are just one of the many groups, or tribes, of Native Americans who live today in North America. There are well over five hundred Native American tribes in the United States and more than six hundred in Canada. At least three million people in North America consider themselves to be Native Americans. But who are Native Americans, and how do the Inuits fit into the history of North America's native peoples?

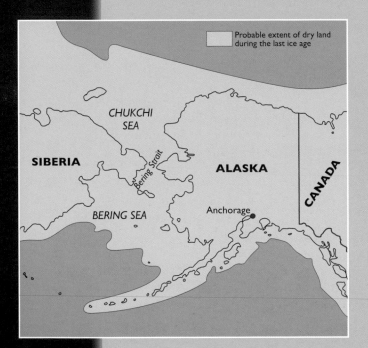

Probable extent of dry land during the last ice age

CHUKCHI SEA

SIBERIA

Bering Strait

ALASKA

CANADA

BERING SEA

Anchorage

Siberia (Asia) and Alaska (North America) are today separated by an area of ocean named the Bering Strait. During the last ice age, the green area on this map was at times dry land. Asian peoples walked from one continent to the other. When the Inuits migrated from Asia thousands of years later they had to travel across the ocean sea ice.

THE FIRST IMMIGRANTS

Native Americans are people whose ancestors settled in North America thousands of years ago. These ancestors may have come from eastern parts of Asia. Their migrations probably occurred during cold periods called **ice ages**. At these times, sea levels were much lower than they are

These people, photographed in 1922, are Yupiks in eastern Siberia (Russia). They are related to the Inuits of North America. Around five thousand years ago, the ancestors of the Inuit left this region and migrated eastward to colonize Arctic North America.

now. The area between northeastern Asia and Alaska was dry land, so it was possible to walk between the continents.

Scientists are not sure when these migrations took place, but it must have been more than twelve thousand years ago. Around that time, water levels rose and covered the land between Asia and the Americas. By around ten thousand years ago, the climate had warmed and was similar to conditions today.

The first peoples in North America moved around the continent in small groups, hunting wild animals and collecting a wide variety of plant foods. Gradually, these groups spread out and lost contact with each other. They developed separate cultures and adopted lifestyles that suited their **environments**. These cultures were very different than those of their original Asian **ancestors**.

The ancestors of the Inuits came to North America from Asia much more recently, possibly five thousand years ago. They must have walked over sea ice or traveled in boats. From Alaska, they

These remains of an Inuit settlement are in Nunavut, Canada, on the northwestern shores of Hudson Bay. The Thule people who lived here from around a thousand years ago were the ancestors of the Inuits.

migrated through northern Canada to Greenland. They always remained in these Arctic and subarctic regions. Although they made trading contact with the Native American tribes to the south, the Inuits never ventured into these regions to settle.

SETTLING DOWN

Many groups of Native Americans to the south continued to gather food and hunt or fish. Others, however, began to live in settlements and grow crops. Their homes ranged from underground pit houses and homes of mud and thatch to dwellings in cliffs. By 3500 B.C., a plentiful supply of fish in the Pacific Ocean and in rivers had enabled people to settle in large coastal villages from Alaska to Washington State. In the deserts of Arizona more than two thousand years later, farmers constructed hundreds of miles of **irrigation** canals to carry water to their crops. In the Mississippi **floodplains**, the Native peoples formed complex societies. They created mud and thatch temples on top of flat earth pyramids. Their largest town, Cahokia, in Illinois, contained more than one hundred mounds and may have been home to 30,000 people.

INUIT LIFE

For the Inuit people in the frozen Arctic, life was very different. They built their homes of stones and driftwood or of blocks of ice. For food they hunted herds of caribou or sea mammals such as whales and seals. The skins of these animals were used to make clothes, summer tents, and tools. Their lifestyle was **nomadic**, as they followed the herds during their annual migrations. Their culture barely changed from that of their Asian ancestors, who continue to live in parts of Northern Siberia, living similar lives to the Inuit.

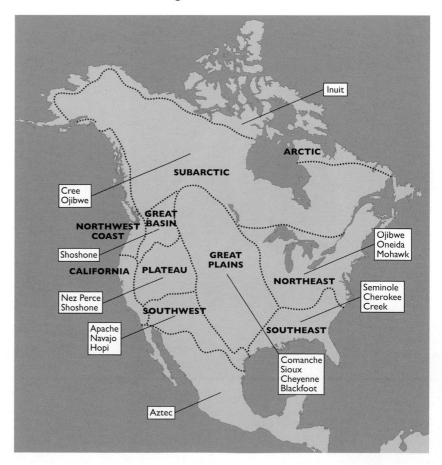

This map of North America highlights the main Native American cultural groups, along with the smaller groups, or tribes, featured in this series of books.

7

Chapter 1

LAND AND ORIGINS

THE PEOPLE CALLED INUIT

The Inuit homelands in North America include northern parts of Canada, Alaska, and the eastern and western coasts of Greenland. A small number of Inuits also live in Siberia. The total Inuit population today is about 155,000.

Some Inuit groups have different names for themselves. The Native American people of Arctic Canada and West Greenland call themselves *Inuit*. Other names are *Inupiat*, *Yupik*, and *Inuvialut*.

All these names mean "people" or "real people." In 1977, representatives from the various Inuit groups met in Alaska and decided they would use *Inuit* to describe all the different groups.

THE INUIT ORIGIN STORY

No one knows for sure how the Inuits came to their homelands. As we have seen, scientists believe that the Inuits came from Asia. However, most of the Inuit groups tell their own origin story. In the distant past, a young girl was forced to marry a man who was really

The Inuits wear jackets called **parkas**. Inuit parkas once had pointy hoods, supposedly so people could easily grab someone who fell through the ice into freezing water.

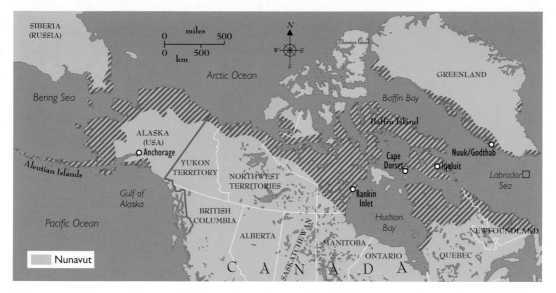

The orange area shows the Inuits' traditional lands. In some places, the Canadian territory of Nunavut, the Inuits' modern homeland indicated in yellow, overlaps their traditional lands. The cities and towns shown have large Inuit populations.

a dog. When they had children, half were human and half were puppies. The mother put the puppies into one shoe and the children into another. The shoes turned into boats that carried their passengers to new homes. The children grew up to become the Inuits. The puppies sailed much farther away, and they became the white Europeans who later explored the Inuits' Arctic homelands.

The Language of the Inuits

There are several Inuit languages, but most speakers can usually understand each other. The following words are in Inuktitut, the language of the eastern Arctic:

Inuit	Pronunciation	English
Ii	ee	yes
aakka	ah-kah	no
qujannamiik	coo-yan-nah-mee-ick	thank you
Iiaali	ee-lah-lih	you're welcome
ikajunga	ick-a-yung-ga	help
tavvauvutit	tah-vow-voo-teet	goodbye

Chapter 2

The Arctic tundra is similar to a desert because it receives little rainfall each year and few plants can grow there. Just four hundred people live year-round on Canada's Ellesmere Island, shown here in late winter.

EARLY ARCTIC DWELLERS

The first people to live in the Arctic **tundra** of North America are sometimes called Paleoeskimos. *Paleo* means "ancient," and *Eskimo* was the name European explorers gave the Inuits. The name came from an Algonquian Indian word referring to snowshoes — not to eating raw meat, as some people once thought.

The Paleoeskimos included the Dorset and Thule (TOO-lee) peoples. The Dorsets first appeared in northern Alaska about five thousand years ago. They then moved eastward into Canada and Greenland, living along the coast.

THE THULES

About twelve hundred years ago, a new **culture** developed in Alaska. The people who created it are known today as the Thule people. The Thules were skillful sailors and hunters, tracking down sea mammals that lived far from the coast.

This photo from the late nineteenth or early twentieth century shows an Inuit husband and wife. In the past, Inuit parents sometimes chose their children's future spouses while they were infants.

Traveling mostly by water, the Thules followed the Dorsets eastward across North America, sailing through the many islands of northern Canada. No one knows why the Dorsets fled or died off as the Thules took over their lands. The Thules were the ancestors of today's Inuits in North America; their languages and culture come from the Thules.

EUROPEANS AND THE THULES

In A.D. 985, a group of **Norse** settlers sailed from Iceland to Greenland. The Thules arrived in Greenland shortly after the Norse. By at least 1200, the Europeans and the Thules had discovered each other and began to trade goods. Over time, however, the Norse disappeared from Greenland, while the Thules spread out along the coast. Inuit tales say the Thules killed the Norse. Scientists think changes in the climate may have made it impossible for the Norse to survive in Greenland.

Following Food

The Thules most likely began to move out of Alaska searching for food. About A.D. 900, the temperature in the Arctic began to rise slowly. As the ice in Arctic waters began to melt, whales began moving eastward, and the Thules followed, because the whales provided most of the Thules' food.

THE AGE OF EXPLORATION

Starting in the fifteenth century, several European nations sent ships to explore the world. In the late sixteenth century, European sea captains thought they could sail through the Arctic Ocean and reach China. They called this supposed shortcut to Asia the Northwest Passage; their search for it led to the first contact between Europeans and the Inuits of Canada.

In 1576, English explorer Martin Frobisher reached Baffin Island in northern Canada while looking for the Northwest Passage. He met some Inuits and took one back with him to England. Hoping to start a colony in Canada, Frobisher returned the next year, but the ice and cold made life too difficult for the settlers who traveled with him. Over the next century, other Europeans continued to sail into Canada's Arctic region, looking for the Northwest Passage. Like Frobisher, they made limited contact with the Inuits.

TRADING GOODS

By the early eighteenth century, the French and British met more Inuits in Canada. From the west, Russians came to North America a little later, exploring and settling in Alaska. By the early nineteenth century, the Russians had made contact with the Inuits, after earlier dealing with the Aleut people, who were distantly related to the Inuits.

The Europeans in Alaska and Canada sought animal furs and skins, which were used for clothing and fashionable beaver-skin hats. The French, British, and Russians all set up trading posts in remote areas and encouraged the Inuits to swap furs and skins for tools, guns, and other items. The Europeans also came to the Arctic to hunt whales. These sea mammals provided the oil used in lamps, whalebones used in women's clothing, and other materials. The sailors on the whaling ships also traded with the Inuits.

In this seventeenth-century painting, European explorers and Canadian Inuits battle. Few Europeans reached the center of the Canadian Arctic until the nineteenth century.

An Unexpected Trip

On his 1576 voyage to Baffin Island, Martin Frobisher captured an Inuit hunter. The English captain hoped the man could help him understand the Inuit language.

During Frobisher's second voyage, in 1577, the English battled the Inuits. After his men killed several Inuits, Frobisher took two more Inuits — a woman and her child — on board his ship. He then returned home with his captives. In England, the Inuit man demonstrated how he hunted with a spear and paddled his **kayak**. He and the other two Inuits died within a month of reaching England, probably from **pneumonia**.

These hunters would have eaten almost every part of the seal they just killed. The Inuits ate seal meat raw, boiled, frozen, and dried.

CHANGES IN INUIT LIFE

In general, the Europeans lacked the Inuits' skills for surviving in the harsh Arctic climate. Through their trading posts and whaling ports, however, the Europeans influenced how the Inuits lived. More Inuits focused on the fur trade. With more frequent contact with Europeans, these Inuits began to rely more on European goods and less on traditional tools and ways of life.

The arrival of the Europeans also led to problems among the Inuits. During the nineteenth century, European diseases spread among the Inuits for the first time, killing many of them. Other Inuits developed **alcoholism** after the Europeans began trading them alcohol for their furs. Whalers killed so many whales that their numbers fell, threatening a key Inuit food source.

The Europeans also tried to change the Inuits' traditional religious beliefs. In Alaska, **missionaries** from the Russian Orthodox Church taught the Inuits the Christian religion. Protestant missionaries from England did the same in parts of Canada. Some Inuits accepted the Europeans'

Today, some Inuits in Alaska still go to Russian Orthodox churches. The word *orthodox* means "right belief."

faith. Others became Christian while still following some of their old religious traditions. The missionaries provided medical care for the Inuits and taught them European languages.

ARCTIC EXPLORATION

Inuits played a key role for Europeans exploring the farthest reaches of the Arctic Circle. During one **expedition** in 1871, four Inuits helped European sailors survive a shipwreck off Greenland. The Inuits built **igloos** for the sailors and hunted for their food. Later explorers, such as Robert Edwin Peary, copied Inuit clothing, traveling methods, and hunting techniques and used the Inuits as guides. With Inuit help, Peary, an American, became one of the first people to reach the North Pole.

U.S. explorer Robert Edwin Peary reached the North Pole in 1909 with four Inuits. He began the trip with twenty-four men, nineteen sledges, and 130 dogs.

Travels with Peary

Although Robert Peary relied on the Inuits for help, he did not always treat them well. A Greenland Inuit named Minik Wallace described his experiences during a trip he and other Inuits took with Peary to New York in 1897:

We were crowded into the hold of the vessel and treated like dogs. Peary seldom came near us. When we reached the end of the sea voyage we were given the most miserable and unhealthy quarters on the steamship *Kite*. . . . [In] the Museum of Natural History in New York . . . we were quartered in a damp cellar most unfavourable to people from the dry air of the North. One after another we became ill and began to die off.

LATER INUIT LIFE

During the twentieth century, Canada, the United States, and Denmark controlled the Arctic lands of North America. The governments of these countries promoted education and assimilation — the process of forcing the Inuits to accept U.S. and European culture.

In the past, most Inuits **migrated** between summer and winter hunting or fishing grounds. Under **Western** influence, they began to settle in permanent communities. By the 1960s and 1970s, more Inuits had indoor plumbing and electricity. Some Inuits also took on jobs at businesses set up by Canadian and U.S. companies. In Alaska, for example, the discovery of oil and the growth of the salmon fishing industry created jobs.

This Inuit village on Little Diomede Island, Alaska, was once a spring hunting site, but residents now live there year-round. In the local language, the village is called Inalik.

POLITICAL ACTIVITIES

In 1924, the Inuits of Alaska became U.S. citizens. In 1959, Alaska became the forty-ninth state. Inuits and other Alaskans could now elect people to represent them in the U.S. Congress.

By that time, most Canadian Inuits lived in a region known as the Northwest Territories. For much of the twentieth century, only some Inuits within the Northwest Territories were represented in Parliament, Canada's lawmaking body. After 1962, the entire region elected a representative to Parliament. The Inuits also had more control over the laws within the Northwest Territories, and Inuits in other parts of Canada also played a larger role in running their own affairs. Starting in 1953, the Inuits of Greenland also won more freedom from the Danish government to control politics in their homeland.

Land Claims in Alaska

The law that made Alaska a state had a large impact on the Inuits. The U.S. government let the state of Alaska claim more than 100 million acres (40 million hectares) of land. The Inuits considered much of this land theirs. In 1966, a group called the Alaska Federation of Natives (AFN) began trying to reclaim this land for the Inuits and other Native Americans in the state. A 1971 U.S. law gave the Native Americans 44 million acres (17.8 million ha) of Alaska's land and almost $1 billion for other lands that they had lost.

In 1971, President Richard Nixon (second from right) met with Donald Wright (right) of the Alaska Federation of Natives to discuss land claims. The AFN represented Aleuts and Native Americans as well as the Inuits.

TRADITIONAL WAY OF LIFE

Chapter 3

DIFFERENT WAYS OF LIFE

Across the Arctic, the Inuits found ways to survive in a cold climate. During the winter, temperatures in some parts of the Arctic can drop below -40° Fahrenheit (-40° Celsius), and the Sun provides almost no light for months at a time. Farming there is impossible so the Inuits became expert at hunting and fishing. During the warmer weather of the brief Arctic summer, the Inuits' lives changed slightly. They could gather nuts, roots, and berries as well as hunt and fish. Because they settled across such a wide region, not all Inuits lived exactly the same way.

THE SEARCH FOR FOOD

During a typical year, most Inuits migrated from one area to another, searching for food. The Copper Inuits of central Canada, for example, hunted seals during the winter, searching for holes in the ice that the seals used to get air. Hunters waited for the seals at the holes, then speared them with **harpoons**. During the summer, the Copper Inuits moved onto land and fished or hunted caribou, musk ox, and other animals.

In other regions, such as Alaska, the Inuits sailed on small boats called umiaks to hunt for large sea mammals, such as walrus and whales, in the spring. Inuits across the Arctic also hunted in kayaks. Similar to canoes, these boats were built for just one person. Both umiaks and kayaks were made of wood and covered with animal skins. In general, most of the whale and walrus hunters also killed bear, fox, rabbit, and duck.

This photo from the early twentieth century shows Alaska Inuit hunters in their umiak. Modern umiaks use motors for power instead of sails and oars.

INUIT HOUSING

In Inuit, the word *iglu* means any kind of home, while the English word *igloo* refers to the famous Inuit snow house. Igloos were most common in the central Arctic, where other building materials were scarce during winter. Some Inuits lined the inside walls with sealskin to help keep their home warm. A hole in the upper wall let in light.

Building an Igloo: An Hour's Work

A nineteenth-century engraving of a typical igloo. The snow inside the igloo slowly melts and refreezes, creating a solid ice wall that makes the igloo sturdy.

Building an igloo took the right conditions and special skill. The snow had to be hard and deep so the builder could use his snow knife to cut large blocks that would not crumble. The builder, usually a man, worked from the inside of his igloo, taking the first blocks from what became part of the floor. When the outer walls were done, the builder's family used soft snow to fill in any gaps between the blocks. Inside, the mother smoothed out the floor and built a platform where the family would sleep.

An Inuit summer home, with a wooden frame and sod roof. In Alaska, the Inuits and their ancestors have used sod houses for thousands of years.

In warmer months, some Inuits dug homes into small hills, adding wooden frames and covering the frames with rock or **sod**. Other Inuits used whalebone frames. Similar to tepees, tents made out of animal skins provided summer homes for some Inuits.

SOCIAL LIFE

The need to migrate meant the Inuits did not build large, permanent towns. Still, the Inuits usually had certain areas where they returned year after year. Several families would form groups called bands, and several bands united to form small communities. The families within a band or community might be related, but often two fathers formed a friendship that united their families. A family or band might decide to leave a certain community after a year or two.

The Inuits did not have formal governments or politics. The men of a community usually made decisions by debating an issue and coming to an agreement. In some regions, an older or very wealthy man might have more influence.

When food was scarce, the communities made sure that everyone received something from a successful hunt. The sharing was most common after killing a large sea mammal, with the largest portions going to the hunters. If food was available, the Inuits would not let someone starve.

These Nunavut Inuits prepare caribou for a local feast, carrying on the tradition of sharing food with all. Caribou remains an important source of food for many Inuits.

FAMILY LIFE

The most important social unit was the nuclear family: a mother, father, and their children. Men hunted, built the homes, and made tools. Women prepared food, raised children, and made clothes from furs and skins, a prized skill since warm clothing was essential for surviving the winter. Women sometimes chewed sealskin to make it soft enough to sew. At times, women also helped fish and gather food for their families.

Most women tied their infants to their body under their large parkas to keep them warm. The babies often went naked, except for a diaper made of caribou skin. As children grew, they learned the skills they would need as adults. At times, they also had chores, such as gathering firewood.

A woman's parka had an oversized hood so it could easily hold an infant. A rope tied around the mother's waist kept the baby in place.

21

THE SPIRIT WORLD

According to traditional Inuit beliefs, the world is filled with spirits. Across the Arctic, the Inuits had different names and ideas about these spirits. In general, the spirits were invisible beings that filled the world. Sometimes they were ghosts of dead people or animals. The Inuits believed these spirits caused most of the illnesses, accidents, and other bad events that trouble humans. The Inuits feared the spirits and did not like to discuss them.

The Inuits also believed that humans had **souls**. Many Inuits thought animals had souls too, and some said everything in the world, including plants and rocks, had souls. The entire universe had a breath-soul commonly called Sila, associated with the air and weather.

While alive, a person had a breath-soul connected to Sila and a free-soul created by three goddesses — the Indweller in the Earth, the Sea Mother, and the Caribou Mother. Only the free-soul survived after a person died, usually traveling on to another world and then entering another human to live again.

THE SHAMAN

At times, the Inuits needed to contact the spirit world, perhaps to end an illness or bring good weather. To communicate with the spirits, the Inuits relied on shamans, people thought to have special skills that would

Shamans wore masks like this during their religious ceremonies. Some masks represented spirits, while others might look like animals.

An Alaskan Inuit shaman tries to heal a sick boy in 1910. The Inuits believed their shamans could drive out evil spirits that caused sickness.

help them contact spirits. The shamans relied on ghosts or helpful spirits to do their work, and they performed ceremonies to talk with the spirit world.

The Inuits believed that shamans could perform miracles such as flying through the air or bringing the dead back to life. The shamans were the Inuits' doctors and sometimes their judges; a shaman might be asked to help settle a dispute. The Inuits also believed shamans could use their powers to curse people they disliked, sometimes leading to their death.

Inuit Myths

The Inuit have a rich tradition of **myths** and legends. Most of these are concerned with the natural world.

MALINA AND ANNINGAN

Malina is the Sun goddess of the Inuit people who live in Greenland, and Anningan is the Moon god. Malina and Anningan used to live together but, one day, they had a terrible argument and began to fight each other. Malina ran away from Anningan far into the sky and became the Sun. Anningan ran after her and became the Moon.

Their chase still continues. Anningan races after his sister day by day. Forgetting to eat, he becomes thinner and thinner until he disappears altogether. (This explains the **phases of the Moon**.) During the time when he is invisible, Anningan eats. Then he reappears to chase his sister once more. Malina tries to stay away from her brother, which is why the Sun and Moon rise and set at different times.

A colorful sunset in Nunavut, Canada. The Inuits believed that this was the Sun goddess Malina escaping before her brother Anningan, the Moon god, appeared in the sky.

Traditionally the Inuits believed that the sea mammals they hunted, such as these harp seals, were descended from the fingers of Sedna, the goddess of the sea.

SEDNA

Sedna is the Sea Mother, or sea goddess, of the Inuits of Greenland and northern Canada. There are many different stories about how she came to live at the bottom of the sea. One is that, as a young girl, she refused to marry any of the young men that her father offered to her.

In the end, she married a dog. Her father was so furious that he tried to throw her into the sea. But Sedna held onto the side of her father's kayak so tightly that he had to cut off her fingers, one by one. Sedna then sank to the bottom of the sea, where she lives today as the goddess of the sea. Her fingers became the seals and other sea animals.

In November 2003, a large planetoid (small planet) was discovered on the cold, outer fringe of our solar system. It was named Sedna after the Inuit goddess, who lives in the cold Arctic regions of our own planet.

Using a hand drill, an artist makes holes in ivory. He spins the drill with a bow and uses a special tool in his mouth to keep the drill in place.

THE CREATIVE INUITS

The Inuits often revealed their artistic talents when they created the tools and other items they needed to survive. Women decorated clothing with leather, furs, and colorful beaded work. Men carved **ivory** decorations worn on clothing or as jewelry. Carvers also engraved images on larger bones or pieces of ivory. Shamans wore masks carved from wood or made of animal fur. Some Inuits in warmer regions made baskets out of coiled grass.

The Inuits also took time to sing, dance, and play music, often with animal-skin drums that looked like tambourines. They held dances to welcome visitors. During the winter, some communities built a large snow house that served as a dance hall. In summer, a large tent was used as the local social center. The Inuits danced and sang while musicians played.

Siberian Inuits in traditional clothes perform a dance. In their dances, the Inuits sometimes act out folktales or copy the movement of animals.

For centuries, the Inuits have enjoyed several kinds of wrestling. Both boys and girls compete in wrestling matches at the Arctic Winter Games, an event similar to the Olympics.

FUN AND GAMES

Inuit social gatherings often featured games and sports, usually designed to test people's strength. Large groups sometimes took part in a tug-of-war, while two men might wrestle or have a punching duel. In this form of boxing, the men took turns hitting each other without trying to avoid their opponent's blows.

Another popular game was *ajagak*, which used a bone drilled with small holes. The bone was tied to a stick, and the player tossed the bone into the air and tried to get the stick into one of the holes. The Inuits also played a version of the fingers-and-string game known as cat's cradle to create animal shapes.

Child's Play

Inuit children had their own toys and games. Kids played hide-and-seek and a game called raven, similar to tag. One child was the hunter while the other players pretended to be ravens trying to escape the hunter. Children also played with dolls made from animal skins or carved from bones.

27

INUIT LIFE TODAY

Chapter 4

OLD AND NEW

Today, most Inuits blend their old customs with modern ways of life. They still go out on the tundra to hunt caribou and seal. Instead of riding on dog sledges, however, they speed across the ice and snow on snowmobiles. Planes provide contact with the outside world, transporting people and supplies. In Inuit towns, people drive **all-terrain vehicles.**

Small houses and log cabins have replaced the tents and sod homes of the past in villages and small towns. In some areas, the Inuits still build igloos as temporary homes while camping or hunting. Since sealskins dry out in heated houses, women in central Canada prefer to work with sealskins used for clothing in snow houses while actually living in framed wooden homes nearby. The Inuits wear the animal skins and furs along with modern clothing.

Snowmobiles are expensive to buy and run, but they help the Inuits travel across the tundra. Many Inuits use them for hunting.

INUIT YOUTH

Most Inuit children go to public schools, and some go on to colleges and universities, which are usually located in larger cities to the south. Over the past few decades, the Inuits have fought to make sure their schools teach students Inuit language and culture. Leaders do not want the students to become totally Western and forget their roots. Now, Inuit schools teach students how to prepare traditional foods and use animal **hides** for clothing. At the same time, the children need to learn about the outside world if they plan to leave their small Arctic communities for larger towns. Television and other media have helped the Inuits learn more about the world beyond the tundra.

Inuit on Ice

In 2003, twenty-year-old Jordin Tootoo made history. Playing for the Nashville Predators, he became the first Inuit to reach the National Hockey League. Tootoo and his family reflect how the Inuits are combining the old and the new. His grandmother was born in an igloo in central Canada, and his uncle raises sled dogs, which are now used mostly for races. Tootoo learned to hunt seal with a harpoon, yet he easily surfs the Internet. With his professional hockey career, Tootoo has a chance to travel that few Inuits get. His goal is to one day bring the Stanley Cup, hockey's championship trophy, home to his village.

Jordin Tootoo (right) celebrates his first National Hockey League (NHL) goal.

An Inuit artist prepares to make a print. Some Inuit printmakers in Cape Dorset, Canada, cut an image into stone, apply ink to the image, then make their prints.

INUITS AT WORK

Many Inuits earn their income by traditional methods, such as trapping animals for their furs and fishing. In some areas, Inuits work in the mining or oil industries. Inuits also work in their communities as teachers, police officers, store clerks and managers, and government officials.

CREATIVE LIFESTYLES

Some Inuits make their livings in the arts. Inuit artists sculpt, paint, and make prints, often showing scenes of Arctic life. Many mix modern techniques with traditional Inuit art forms. World famous for his work in stone, ivory, and other materials, Osuitok Ipeelee (1922–2005) of Nunavut, the Inuits' modern homeland in Canada, began carving in the 1940s. His subjects included traditional Inuit images such as birds, seals, and caribou. Another well-known carver is Oviloo Tunnillie, a Nunavut Inuit who now spends her time in Ottawa and Montreal, Canada. Tunnillie is best known for her female figures. She comes from a family of artists. Her father Toonoo was one of the first successful Inuit sculptors.

Inuit writers, working in both Native and European languages, are reporters and novelists. Some write down ancient Inuit folktales, while others examine how the Inuits live in the modern world. Mitiarjuk Attasie Nappaaluk (1931–2007) wrote *Sanaaq*, the first novel in the Inuktitut language. Her story looks at Inuit life from a female point of view.

In 2001, a group of Canadian Inuit filmmakers wrote and produced the first full-length movie ever made in an Inuit language, *Atanarjuat* (The Fast Runner). The story of the movie was based on an ancient Inuit legend. In 2010, the movie *Le Voyage d'Inuk* was premiered. In this movie, a teenage Inuit boy from the city is sent to a children's home in the far north and learns about traditional seal hunting. The whole cast were local Greenland Inuits, who had never acted before.

Throat Singing

The Inuits enjoy singing accompanied by drumming and dancers. However, among the Canadian Inuit, another more unusual type of singing is also very popular. This is throat singing, in which two women face each other and alternate in making rhythmic, deep, breathy sounds. It is like a game or competition. One person begins with a short rhythmic repeated phrase, while the other person fills in the gaps. The one who can continue singing for the longest time wins.

Tanya Tagaq is a modern throat singer who has developed a new solo style. She is very popular both in Canada and abroad and has produced several albums.

HUNTING FOR A LIVING

Not all Inuits can make a living as they choose. In Alaska, whalers face limits on the number of bowhead whales they can

kill. International groups worry that the bowheads will disappear, because so many of them have been killed over the centuries—mostly by nineteenth-century American and European whalers. The limits on whale hunting anger many Inuits, who argue that they should not be denied their traditional source of food because of the Western whale kills of years ago.

Traditional ways of life endure in Nunavut. Here, a fisherman catches Arctic char in a frozen lake.

The Eskimo Scouts

Since Alaska came under U.S. control in 1867, some Inuits have worked for the U.S. military. During World War II, about six thousand Inuits, both men and women, watched for a possible enemy invasion; they were nicknamed the Eskimo Scouts. After the war, many of the Inuits joined the Alaska National Guard, and the old nickname endured. The Eskimo Scouts often trained U.S. soldiers, teaching them how to fight and survive in Arctic regions. Today, the Eskimo Scouts serve in the war on terrorism, watching for potential attacks against Alaska's oil pipelines, seaports, and airports.

Hunting and fishing remain important to the Inuits because most food is expensive in the Arctic. Anything from outside the region must be brought on planes or ships.

HEALTH PROBLEMS

Over the last few decades, many Inuits have developed serious illnesses related to their lifestyles and their environment. A recent survey showed that **obesity**, tooth decay, **diabetes**, heart disease, high blood pressure, and cancer were all much more common than they were thirty years ago.

One of the reasons for this ill health is a change in the Inuit diet. Today the Inuits eat less fresh local meat and buy more high-calorie fast foods and beverages, which have very little nutritional value. The meat and fish the Inuits traditionally ate was good for their hearts, and the exercise of hunting and fishing also kept them healthy. As they exchanged a hunting lifestyle for less active jobs, many Inuits have developed diseases that are common in other parts of North America. They are also becoming shortsighted. Some experts think this may also be related to diet, while others believe it is caused by reading and computer use.

These Inuit children are consuming unhealthy imported foods and beverages rather than traditional meats. Because of this change of diet, the Inuits are now experiencing health problems similar to people in other parts of North America who also eat a lot of fast food.

Another reason for Inuit ill health is that many Inuits smoke, drink too much alcohol, and take drugs. Many of them have found it difficult to adjust to a new way of living and have lost their sense of identity. This has led to depression and, in some cases, suicide.

POISON IN THE ENVIRONMENT

Over recent years, poisonous chemicals from industrial processes have entered the Arctic Ocean. These chemicals are taken up by animals and remain in their stored fat. As these animals are eaten by larger animals, the poisons collect in the fat of these predators. Finally, these meat-eating animals are hunted by the Inuits, who eat the fat and suffer from the effects of these poisons.

CLIMATE CHANGE

As the world warms up, ice in the Arctic region melts. This is a particular problem for the Inuits. They know that if warming continues it will mean the end of their traditional life. All the Inuit groups in Alaska, Canada, and Greenland are joining together to express concern about **global warming**.

Already the Inuits can no longer predict when the ice will arrive in winter or melt in spring. Winters have become shorter, and sometimes rain falls instead of snow. In Baffin Island, Canada, flash floods have already washed away soil, even exposing the rocks beneath.

Melting ice makes finding animal prey more difficult for Inuit hunters. They can no longer be sure where the animals can be found. They also risk falling through thin ice as they hunt.

Another result of warming is the melting of the **permafrost** in the ground. The ground becomes unstable and the foundations of buildings, roads, and runways collapse. Even the seashore is **eroded**. Harbors fall apart and people have to move inland. At the moment, no one can predict how warmer oceans will affect the lives and migrations of the sea and land mammals that the Inuits hunt.

> My core message is that we are all connected. The Arctic is geographically isolated from the rest of the world, yet the Inuk [Inuit] hunter who falls through the thinning sea ice is connected to melting glaciers in the Andes and the Himalayas, and to the flooding of low-lying and small island states.
> *Sheila Watt-Cloutier*

Sheila Watt-Cloutier

Born in an Inuit settlement in Quebec, Canada, in 1953, Sheila Watt-Cloutier experienced a traditional Inuit early childhood. For many years she worked to improve Inuit education. Then in 1998 she was elected Canadian president of the Inuit Circumpolar Council (ICC), which represents all Inuit groups.

Sheila Watt-Cloutier lived a traditional Inuit life until she was sent away to school at ten years of age. Today she campaigns to preserve Inuit lifestyles in the face of climate change and ocean **pollution**.

As a spokesperson for Inuit peoples she spoke out against the production and use of poisonous chemicals that were entering the Arctic food chain. Now, many of these chemicals are banned. Recently, Watt-Cloutier has spoken out worldwide against global warming, explaining how it affects the Inuits. She stresses that what is happening to the Inuits is a warning of future changes across the world.

Chapter 5

AN INUIT HOMELAND

A Nunavut mother and son stand next to a stone sculpture called an *inuksuk*. An inuksuk can be thousands of years old and might mark a path or warn of dangerous conditions. An inuksuk was used as the logo of the Vancouver 2010 Winter Olympics.

Over the last few decades, the Inuits have tried to make sure the governments that control their lands do not ignore them or take away their rights.

In 2002, the Alaskan Inuits convinced an international whaling organization to raise the limit on the number of bowhead whales they could kill. The next year, the Inuits of Greenland won a court case that required the Danish government to give them money for forcing them from their homes years before.

NUNAVIK

In the 1960s, the Quebec Inuits, who live in fourteen villages in northern Quebec province, Canada, objected to business plans to use their land for mining, forestry, and **hydroelectricity** developments. They took their case to court, forcing the Quebec and Canadian governments to negotiate with them. This led in 1978 to an agreement in which the Inuit were paid **compensation**. They also gained limited self-government, with powers over health and education. The Quebec Inuits will soon have more self-government in Nunavik ("place to live"), their homeland.

NUNAVUT

In 1999, the Canadian government turned a large portion of the Northwest Territories into a homeland for the Inuits called Nunavut ("our land"). About 29,000 people, mostly Inuits, live in this huge territory, which covers about 772,200 square miles (2 million square kilometers), an area larger than Alaska.

Inuits celebrate the creation of Nunavut in 1999 by displaying the new Nunavut flag, which has an inuksuk in the center.

Inuits walk past the assembly building in Iqaluit. Nunavut's capital has expanded rapidly since 1999. It is now Canada's fastest growing community.

Two Inuit languages are spoken in Nunavut as well as Canada's two official languages, English and French. The territory has just twenty-six communities, and the capital, Iqaluit, has a population of about six thousand. Towns are isolated, with no roads connecting them. The people must fly or sail to travel across the territory.

The creation of Nunavut gave the Inuits of the region local political control. The Nunavut government consists of nineteen elected members. There is also a council of advisors whose job is to make sure that traditional Inuit culture and knowledge are part of government decisions. The government meets in a new assembly building in Iqaluit.

Inuit Broadcasting Corporation

Created in 1982, the Inuit Broadcasting Corporation is run by Inuits who provide television programs in the Inuktituk language. These programs are all about the Inuits and issues that affect them. For instance, some programs are aimed at young children and teach them Inuit values and language. Programs for teenagers teach life skills and look at the problems of being caught between two different cultures. There are also regular phone-ins about issues in the news.

NUNATSIAVUT

After Nunavut was created, the only Inuits in Canada without any self-government were those in the province of Labrador. That changed in 2005, when the Government of Nunatsiavut ("our beautiful land") was created. Its elected members can make new laws about Inuit education, health and culture.

MOVING FORWARD

For thousands of years, the Inuits and their ancestors have lived in one of the most isolated regions of the world. They developed skills and knowledge that made life possible in a harsh climate. With the arrival of Europeans, the Inuit life changed forever. However, the Inuits have found a way to keep their traditions while adjusting to the demands of a different culture.

Inuit Circumpolar Council

The different Inuit groups often work together to reach their goals. In 1977, the Yupik people of Alaska and the Inuits of Canada, Alaska, and Greenland formed the Inuit Circumpolar Council (ICC). Yupik people from eastern Russia later joined the group. The ICC addresses issues that concern all 150,000 Inuits and Yupiks. These include keeping pollution out of the Arctic, promoting traditional culture, creating Inuit-owned businesses, and guaranteeing the Inuits equal rights.

Inuits in northern Alaska celebrate the end of the whale hunting season with a thanksgiving festival named Nalukataq. People feast on whale meat, toss each other in the air on sealskin blankets, and then enjoy a traditional dance.

TIMELINE

about 3000 B.C.	Asian peoples arrive in northern Alaska. They become known later as the Dorset culture.
A.D. 900s	A warmer climate in the Arctic forces the Thule Inuits to move eastward in search of whales to hunt. The Thules, ancestors of the Inuits, begin to move out of northern Alaska and spread eastward along the Arctic Circle.
about 1200	The Thules make contact with the Norse in Greenland.
1300s–1600s	A colder climate forces Inuits to retreat from the high Arctic southward to the edges of the timberline.
1576–1577	Explorer Martin Frobisher takes three Baffin Island Inuits to England; all three die shortly afterward.
1700s	British and French explorers and traders make contact with Canadian Inuits.
late 1700s	Christian missionaries begin to convert Inuits to Christianity.
early 1800s	A Russian fur company trades with Alaskan Inuits.
1840s	U.S. whaling ships begin operating off the Alaskan coast, severely reducing the whale population upon which the Inuits depend.
1867	The United States purchases Alaska from Russia.
1924	Alaskan Inuits become U.S. citizens.
1941–45	Inuit "Eskimo Scouts" in Alaska watch for possible enemy attacks during World War II.
1953	Greenland Inuits begin to win more local political freedom from Denmark.
1959	Alaska becomes the forty-ninth U.S. state, allowing Inuits to vote for representatives in the U.S. government.

1962   All Inuits of Canada's Northwest Territories are allowed to vote for a representative in Parliament.

1970   The first Arctic Winter Games take place, featuring Inuit sports.

early 1970s   Inuit political groups are formed.

1971   U.S. law gives Native Americans in Alaska large areas of land and money as compensation for land taken away.

1977   Inuits across the Arctic form the Inuit Circumpolar Conference to work on issues concerning all Inuits.

1978   Settlement of land claims between the Quebec Inuits and local and national governments. Kativik regional government established.

1979   Greenland Inuits are granted self-rule by Denmark.

1982   The Inuit Broadcasting Corporation is created.

1984   Settlement of land claims between the western Canadian Inuits (Inuvialuits) and Canadian local and national governments.

1999   Canada forms the territory of Nunavut, which is controlled by the region's Inuit population.

2001   *Atanarjuat,* the first feature film in an Inuit language, is made.

2002   Alaskan Inuit whalers win the right to kill more bowhead whales.

2003   Jordin Tootoo is the first Inuit to play in the National Hockey League.

2005   Settlement of land claims between the Labrador Inuits and Canadian local and national governments. Labrador Inuit territory of Nunatsiavut established.

2010   An inuksuk is used as the logo of the Winter Olympics in Vancouver, Canada. *Le voyage d'Inuk*, a feature film about and performed by Greenland Inuits, is released.

GLOSSARY

alcoholism: a disease in which people's desire to drink alcohol is so strong they cannot control it.

all-terrain vehicles: small, open, four-wheeled vehicles with large tires that can move easily over ice and snow.

ancestors: people from whom an individual or group is descended.

Arctic: the cold regions south of the north pole reaching as far as an imaginary line named the Arctic Circle.

compensation: money given to people in return for a loss, such as loss of Native American land.

culture: the arts, beliefs, and customs that make up a people's way of life.

diabetes: a disease in which there is a lack of a sugar-controlling chemical named insulin in the human body.

environment: objects and conditions all around that affect living things and communities.

eroded: worn away by water, wind, or ice.

expedition: a trip taken for a specific reason, such as to explore an unknown area.

floodplain: the area of land beside a river or stream that is covered with water during a flood.

global warming: an increase in the temperature of the air and the oceans.

harpoons: spears with ropes attached so the throwers can pull their catch toward them.

hides: the skins of animals.

hydroelectricity: electricity produced by waterpower.

ice age: a period of time when the earth is very cold and lots of water in the oceans turns to ice.

igloos: dome-shaped dwellings built of blocks of hardened snow.

irrigation: any system for watering the land to grow plants.

ivory: the long tusk, or tooth, of certain mammals such as a walrus.

kayak: a long, thin canoe usually built for one person.

migrated: moved from one area to another.

missionaries: people who try to teach others their religion.

myth: a traditional story that explains beliefs or events in nature.

nomadic: not having a single home but moving from place to place in search of food or following groups of animals.

Norse: describes people from northern Europe, particularly Norway, who settled in Iceland and Greenland.

obesity: having far too much fat stored in the body.

parkas: warm fur jackets with a hood.

permafrost: ice in the ground that never melts because the temperature is too cold.

phases of the Moon: the changes in the appearance of the Moon that are repeated every month.

pneumonia: a serious illness making it difficult for a person to breathe.

pollution: anything made by humans that makes other things dirty or poisons them.

sod: grass or turf.

souls: energies or invisible forces thought to create human life or be connected to gods; also the spiritual part of human beings.

subarctic: the cold regions immediately south of the Arctic.

tundra: a cold region with few or no trees and a layer of soil beneath the surface that always stays frozen.

Western: relating to European and North American culture.

MORE RESOURCES

WEBSITES:

http://epe.lac-bac.gc.ca/100/205/301/ic/cdc/arctic/inuit/people.htm
The Canadian Arctic Profiles: Indigenous Culture website covers the history, communities, beliefs, economy, and hunting techniques of the native peoples.

http://epe.lac-bac.gc.ca/100/205/301/ic/cdc/cape_dorset/index2.html
Interviews with Inuit elders and art from Cape Dorset.

http://library.thinkquest.org/3877/Yupik.html
A site about the Inupiat and Yupik peoples who live in Alaska.

http://www.athropolis.com/news-upload/master/11-frames.htm
An Inuit school project on favorite traditional Inuit games with photos of the games being played.

http://www.elements.nb.ca/kids/snow/snoword.htm
Thirty-one words for snow and their meanings in Inuit languages.

http://www.heritage.nf.ca/aboriginal/prehist.html
The Newfoundland and Labrador Heritage: Aboriginal Peoples website covers local Native American history from 800 B.C. to the recent past.

http://www.mnh.si.edu/arctic/index.html
Smithsonian National Museum of Natural History's Arctic Studies Center explores the history of northern peoples, cultures, environments, and the issues that matter to northern residents today.

http://www.sila.nu/pub/swf/tgah/en/index.html
Play the Great Arctic Hunter game and learn about the habits, habitats, and distribution of the animals the Inuits hunt.

http://www.stuff.co.uk/media/polar-relay/inuit.html
Sound files of Inuit throat singing.

http://www.turtletrack.org/Issues02/Co07132002/CO_07132002_ Nunavut_names.htm
How the Inuits lost their traditional names and are now claiming them back.

DVDs:

Atanarjuat (The Fast Runner). Ica Films, 2009.

Nanook of the North. Criterion Collection, 1998.

BOOKS:

Alexander, Cherry. *Inuit (Flashback History)*. PowerKids Press, 2009.

Houston, James. *James Houston's Treasury of Inuit Legends (Odyssey Classics)*. Harcourt Children's Books, 2006.

Ipellie, Alootook and David MacDonald. *The Inuit Thought of It: Amazing Arctic Innovations (We Thought of It)*. Annick Press, 2007.

Kent, Deborah. *The Inuit: A Proud People (American Indians)*. Enslow Elementary, 2005.

King, David C. *The Inuit (First Americans)*. Benchmark Books, 2007.

Reynolds, Jan. *Frozen Land (Vanishing Cultures)*. Lee & Low Books, 2007.

Rivera, Raquel. *Arctic Adventures: Tales from the Lives of Inuit Artists*. Groundwood Books, 2007.

Rivera, Raquel. *Tuk and the Whale*. Groundwood Books, 2009.

Strudwick, Leslie. *The Inuit (Indigenous Peoples)*. Weigl Publishers, 2004.

Wallace, Mary. *I is for Inuksuk: An Arctic Celebration*. Maple Tree Press, 2009.

Wallace, Mary. *The Inuksuk Book (Wow Canada! Collection)*. Maple Tree Press, 2004.

Wallace, Mary. *Inuksuk Journey: An Artist at the Top of the World*. Maple Tree Press, 2008.

Williams, Suzanne. *The Inuit (Watts Library: Indians of the Americas)*. Franklin Watts, 2004.

THINGS TO THINK ABOUT AND DO

The Weather and You

Find out the average temperature for your state during the winter. How does this compare to the temperatures in the Arctic? Make a list of the ways the weather in your region affects what you do during the winter and summer.

Working Together

Think of a problem in your local community. Who could you work with to try to solve this problem? What people would you have to contact to change the current situation? Would it be more helpful to talk to political leaders, teachers, or other students? Discuss this with other students.

The Need for Nature

What is one animal or natural resource that is important to your community today? How do people use it? What would happen to the community if that resource suddenly disappeared? Write a paragraph with your thoughts.

Build an Igloo

Using sugar cubes, shreds of paper mixed with glue or paste, or other materials, build a model of an igloo. Design the interior and craft the tools of the Inuit hunters such as harpoons and sleds that may be inside or outside the igloo.

INDEX